Adventure in the Zoo!

Mary O'Keeffe

Tom and Ella were on the bus.

Mr Lillis and all of the children were on the bus too.

It was the last Thursday in May.

It was their school tour!

Tom's dad, Sam, came along for the ride.

"The wheels on the bus go round and round!" sang Ella and Anna.

"The teachers on the bus say 'shush, shush, shush!'" chanted Tom and Peter.

When the bus got to the zoo, it came to a stop.

The children got off and waited with their pals to go into the zoo.

"Let's go and see the **animals**!" said Charlie the zookeeper.

First up, it was the African Plains.

This is the cheetah.

Cheetahs are big cats.

They have soft, spotty fur.

Cheetahs hunt during the day.

They have sharp teeth.

They like to chew their food in the shade.

Baby cheetahs are called cubs.

They run very fast.

This is the ostrich.

It is a big bird with lots of big **feathers**.

It shakes its **feathers** when it is mad!

An ostrich has wings, but it cannot fly.

It can run very fast.

An ostrich egg is the biggest egg in the **world**.

Ostriches are wild in Africa.

"Whoa, there's a bit of a whiff over here!" shouted Ella and Tom.

"This is the farm," said Charlie.

"There are goats, cows and pigs here, so it should be a bit smelly!" said Charlie. "You can pet the **animals**, but look out! They could give you a nip!"

The children were on their way to the next part of the zoo.

"Hold on, children. I want to show you my **favourite animal** in the zoo," said Sam.

"Is it a shark?" they all asked.

"No, we're not going near the fish this time," said Sam.

"What is your **favourite animal**, Sam?" asked Charlie.

This is the sloth.

Sloths have thick fur and long arms.

They have long **claws** too.

Sloths live in the jungle in the wild.

They are very slow.

They like to sleep a lot!

"I think that might be my new **favourite animal**, Dad!" said Tom with a grin.

What does it look like? 👀

What does it sound like? 👂

Where does it live? 🏠

What does it eat? 🥣

Why is it your **favourite**?